Old Bournville
Paul Chrystal

Steam and horse-powered vehicles lined up and waiting to go. The first petrol vans were introduced in 1906, so the photo dates after that. Between the van and the horse drawn wagons is a steam waggon.

Acknowledgements

Thanks go to Sarah Foden, Cadbury Archive, Kraft Foods, for permission to use many of the Cadbury images in the book. Thanks too to Diane Thornton, Bournville Village Trust for permission to use the illustration on page 8, originally published in Michael Harrison's *Bournville – Model Village to Garden Suburb*.

© Paul Chrystal, 2015
First published in the United Kingdom, 2015,
by Stenlake Publishing Ltd.
www.stenlake.co.uk
ISBN 9781840337051

Cadbury were the first company to use powered canal boats with their fleet of barges in Cadbury livery.

Introduction

Bournville is a shining example of the industrial model village – that attempt by various industrialists around the world to provide workers with an escape route from the hideous conditions in which they otherwise might have lived. Like New Earswick near York, Saltaire and Port Sunlight, amongst others, Bournville grew out of the shocking conditions in which workers were obliged to toil and subsist during the Industrial Revolution. These villages were the enlightened manifestation of a growing awareness that something had to be done about the chronic overcrowding and the insanitary, disease ridden houses and squalid streets which droves of workers left each dawn for the inhumane factory conditions and relentless, often dangerous, labour which paid their meagre wages. The industrial village concept , however, was never just an expression of altruism, philanthropy or paternalism. The welfare could not exist without a substantial, thriving business to support it, and a profitable business at that. The stark difference between the industrialist who housed his workforce in a model village and worked them in an efficient, relatively safe factory, the difference between him and the average factory owner was that the benefactor, Cadbury, Rowntree, Salt and Lever, to name but a few, had the vision to realise the long-term benefits of reinvesting profits for the betterment of the workers while at the same time benefitting from a stable, more productive, comparatively contented workforce.

One of the earliest expressions of this enlightened, progressive attitude was at New Lanark, in the village developed in the 1780s by David Dale, Richard Arkwright and George Dempster. They harnessed the waters of the River Clyde some 40 km south of Glasgow to power their cotton mills. Their workforce comprised Highlanders dispossessed by the Clearances, and the able-bodied from work houses and orphanages further south; they were accommodated close to the mills; being somewhat isolated, their new community had to be largely self-sufficient. Dale, apart from providing a relatively salubrious place to live with acceptable working conditions, also laid on education for children, unpolluted water, and no sign of the foul mess that often swilled around the workers' homes and streets back in the cities. Dale, however, had not finished: with Claud Alexander he went on to found Catrine on the River Ayr, a model village built around the mill, complete with a river walk, allotments, good housing, a school and sick and industrial accident pay.

Just before 1800 Robert Owen arrived on the scene. He married Dale's daughter and took over New Lanark in 1801. It was a while before he was able to win over the workforce, but over time he successfully developed Dale and Alexander's ideas. Owen is remembered as the father of socialism while the pioneering Dale is largely forgotten.

Meanwhile, good housing for out of town workers (long-distance commuting was not the norm), was being embraced by the Colman mustard family at Trowse near Norwich in 1805. Nenthead in Cumbria followed from 1825 – a village of 2,000 or so people employed by the Quaker London Lead Company in the productive Nenthead Mines. The Quakers built houses, gardens, a school, market hall, a reading room, a ready money shop, an inn, post office, public baths and a washhouse for the miners and their families.

There was similar progress to come: John Grubb Richardson, another Quaker, set up Bessbrook near Newry in 1845 for his linen mill workforce; he was probably influenced by the model village established at Portlaw in County Waterford in 1825 by the Quaker Malcolmson family for their cotton mill workers. Edward Ackroyd built his villages at Copley (1849) and Akroydon (1861) near Halifax, encouraging home-ownership and laying the foundations for the Halifax Building Society. Meanwhile, Ironbridge for the Butterley Iron Company, Bromborough Pool on the Wirral for Price's Patent Candle Company, Meltham Mills near Huddersfield set up by Jonas Brook for the 1,000 strong workforce at his silk mills; Swindon railway village – all of these and others were realised in the mid 1800s.

Saltaire was the first British model village of any size to serve an individual industrial concern. The impulse came from a desire to achieve efficiencies on the shop floor with efficient, safe plant and a contented workforce – in short to maximise profits while satisfying a desire to improve the social and industrial welfare of his workers. Bournville for the Cadbury workers, Port Sunlight for the Lever workforce and New Earswick near York – a mixed community for Rowntree workers and others – all followed.

The model industrial garden village movement received something of a boost when the short-lived Society for Promoting Industrial Villages was established in 1883 with Lord Shaftesbury as one of its vice presidents. It had no real authority but it did conveniently lay down and formalise what a garden village should comprise. Further impetus came when Ebenezer Howard published his *Tomorrow* in 1898; the second edition in 1902 was retitled *Garden Cities of Tomorrow*. In it, Howard condensed the best features

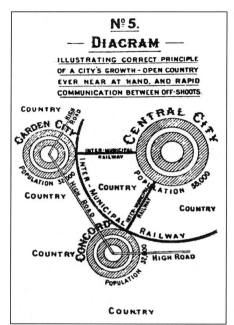

of each of the earlier reformers to produce a blueprint for an achievable 'town-country' garden city. The diagrams on this page show the zoning which demarcates working and living spaces with varied housing, parks, public social buildings, street layouts and surrounding horticultural and agricultural land. The essential difference between Howard and what came before and, indeed, after, was that Howard's village assumed no factory, no workforce to populate the settlement and no rich benefactor. Howard overcame this by raising capital through his First Garden City Limited, the business end of the Garden City Association, from which Letchworth Garden City was later built.

The story of Bournville and Cadbury would be quite incomplete without reference to the Quaker leanings of Cadbury and other social benefactors of the time. Quakerism had a profound influence on their attitude to industrial relations, living and working conditions and workers' benefits. For Fry in Bristol, Quaker sentiments drove the move to the rural and ergonomic factory at Somerdale. For Cadbury it was responsible for the same enlightened approach to employees and a similar 'factory in a garden' ideal. Here, though (as later in Rowntree's New Earswick), it was augmented by a fine new garden village at Bournville which allowed workers to live in relative comfort, enjoying levels of hygiene and health rarely seen in the urban slums from which the workers were lifted. Sport and social activities and education were all paramount, as were progressive employee benefits that were years ahead of most other companies.

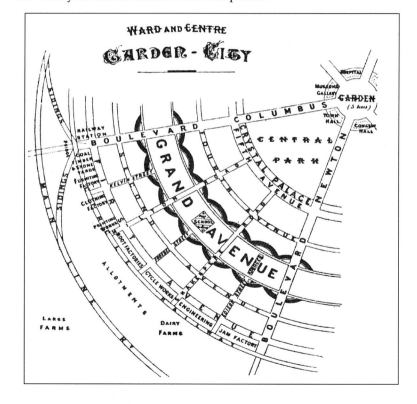

In the early years of the 20th century there were industry-led developments at, for example, Woodlands Colliery Village near Doncaster in 1905 where provision was made for 1,000 houses for miners and their families, and at New Earswick which was administered by one of the Joseph Rowntree Trusts from 1904 , as it still is to this day. In 1908 Reckitt's, the Quaker Hull chemical and cleaning materials company, built 400 houses which formed the Hull Garden suburb for some of its 3,300 employees.

Britain, of course, was not alone. There were similar settlements overseas: in Europe, for example, at Crespi d'Adda in Lombardy, Cristoforo Crespi built his village around his cotton mill from 1878; in 1874 Noisiel east of Paris was founded to house some of the 2,000 employees working at the Chocolat Menier chocolate factory, one of Europe's biggest confectionery companies, far bigger than Cadbury's, Fry's and Rowntree at the time. Later, in 1938 Stadt des KdF-Wagens bei Fallersleben (later Wolfsburg) was built to provide a settlement for workers at the Volkswagen factory manufacturing the KdF-Wagen or VW Beetle.

In 1824 John Cadbury, son of a prosperous Quaker, set up his shop selling tea, coffee and sixteen varieties of drinking chocolate – at 93 Bull Street, Birmingham after completing an apprenticeship in London at the Sanderson, Fox & Company teahouse. The shop was certainly remarkable: it featured an eye-catching window filled with Chinese vases and figures and, appropriately for a tea merchants, a Chinese shop assistant dressed in full Chinese regalia. The picture shows it as it was in the 1830s. Cadbury then moved to an old malt house in Crooked Lane where he perfected cocoa bean grinding, and then to a factory in Bridge Street. John's brother, Benjamin, joined and the company became known as Cadbury Brothers of Birmingham. John Cadbury's sons, Richard and George, took over the business in 1861 – still modest with about ten employees and not at all successful. George joined in 1857 after a three year apprenticeship with Rowntrees' grocery business in Pavement, York. Back on the shop floor in the mid 1800s, things were not going well, that is until George's 1866 visit to Coenraad van Houten to acquire one of his revolutionary presses which revolutionised the production of chocolate; this visit was pivotal and eventually led the way from a company teetering on the brink of failure to the successful company it was soon to become.

This image was first published in *Bournville – The Factory in a Garden* – a booklet given to the many visitors to the Cadbury factory down the years; it epitomises the Cadburys' aims and aspirations for their factory and the village and was reproduced from the mural in the Visitor's Tea Room. It shows George and Richard Cadbury at the brand new factory in discussion with George Gadd, the Bournville architect, about the next stage: the building of the village which '*must have gardens to be complete*'. The deeds he handed over to the Bournville Village Trust in 1900 leave no doubt about George Cadbury's intentions and objectives: '*The Founder is desirous of alleviating the evils which arise from the insanitary and insufficient accommodation supplied to the large numbers of the working classes, and to securing to workers in the factories some of the advantages of outdoor village life, with opportunities for the natural and healthful occupation of cultivating the soil … by the provision of improved dwellings, with gardens and open spaces to be enjoyed therewith.*'

A page from *Sixty Years of Planning: The Bournville Experiment* published during the Second World War; it shows early building in 1879 with architect George Gadd on the right. George Cadbury bought a further 120 acres of land next to his factory in 1893 on which to build his model village. This was inspired by what he saw all around him in the centre of Birmingham: '*It is not easy to describe or imagine the dreary desolation which acre after acre of the very heart of the town presents...hundreds of leaky, damp, wretched houses, wholly unfit for human habitation*'. At first the houses were intended just for Cadbury employees but this exclusivity was later abandoned in favour of a design to create a village of mixed housing for a wide range of inhabitants, thereby establishing a mixed community at Bournville; Bournville in effect was a full scale community planning project. During construction of the factory sixteen good sized cottages were constructed for key workers. In 1895 more land was bought, the architect Alexander Harvey was engaged and the following year building began. On Bournville Building Estate rules were laid down: each house was to occupy no more than a quarter of its building plot and each garden was to be "not less than one-sixth of an acre" with at least six fruit trees. By 1905 315 houses had been built. In 1906 a workers' housing co-operative, Bournville Tenants Limited, leased building land and added another 398 houses. In 1913 a model garden suburb for white-collar workers was built. In the 1920s and 1930s a number of co-operatives and societies expanded the village through independent arrangements. In 1930 the "Sunshine Homes" were built, sited and laid out so that they each caught the maximum amount of sunlight. From 1950-1962 The Trust and the City Housing Department constructed a new development with shops and churches which became part of Shenley Fields. By the 1960s and 1970s a number of special-needs schemes included houses built specifically for the elderly and the visually impaired.

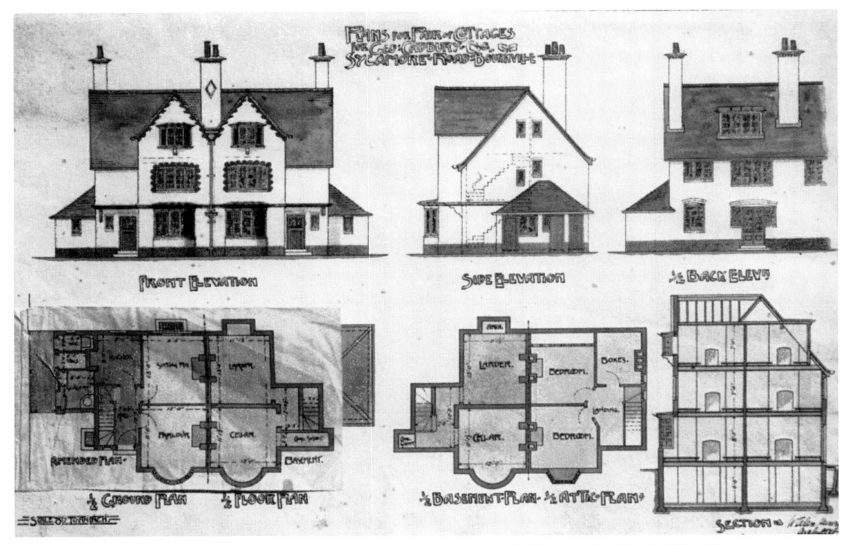

The illustrations here show the plans for 13-15 Sycamore Road published in *Bournville: Model Village to Garden Suburb* by Michael Harrison.

8

All Bournville houses came with a bath – in a separate bathroom in the larger houses, in the kitchen in the smaller houses. The Patent Adjustable Cabinet Bath – raised and lowered from a fitted cupboard – was the most popular; other types included the Sunken Bath (in the floor) and the Table Bath which comprised a bath covered with a removable work surface. Top of the range was probably the Cornes' Combined Scullery-Bath Range and Boiler – very economic in its shared use of heat. The picture was originally published in *Sixty Years of Planning: The Bournville Experiment*.

A postcard showing the men's recreation grounds with the fishing pool in the foreground and the school in the background; yachting was available in the Valley Pool. At one time the Model Yacht Club had over 100 members and was one of the biggest in the country, with its own Commodore.

This postcard shows the men's pavilion which was donated in 1902 to commemorate the coronation of Edward VII, complete with gym, showers and changing rooms, and the recreation grounds – home to one of the finest cricket grounds in the Midlands and to Arthur Lilley of Warwickshire and JB Lilley, captain of Worcestershire.

Boys enjoyed a wide range of in-service apprenticeships while girls had the sewing club. Employees were, as a matter of course, treated with respect. The works councils, segregated until 1964, comprised management and shop floor representatives and were primarily responsible for the company's welfare schemes. This photo shows the workforce enjoying one of the regular lunch-time concerts.

An indoor swimming pool was opened in Bournville Lane; all the sports facilities were free of charge. The photograph (first published in *A Century of Progress 1831-1931*) shows the girls' baths which were built in 1905: 80 feet by 46 feet with a capacity of 105,000 gallons; 87 dressing boxes, 27 spray baths. Swimming lessons here taught thousands of girls how to swim.

Bourneville Girls Playing Net Ball.

Rowheath was bought to accommodate football and hockey pitches and an athletics track. The Pavilion opened in 1924 as a clubhouse and changing facility for the sportsmen and as a venue for dinners and dances. There were also bowling greens, a fishing lake and an outdoor lido. The pictures show girls playing netball in the girls' recreation ground which also had a hockey pitch and tennis courts. The Girls' Athletic Club had 113 members in 1899.

To complete the superb sports facilities available to Bournville village residents, the factory laid on physical exercise classes, as the girls show here posing in 1902. The photograph first appeared in *A Century of Progress 1831-1931*.

Bournville Day Continuation School opened in 1925, the aim being to further the education of Cadbury employees. Attendance was compulsory for everyone between the ages of fourteen to eighteen; male clerks attended for an extra year and apprentices until they were twenty-one. Lessons in English, maths and science were complemented with physical education and handicrafts. Continuation Classes were held in this purpose-built building comprising 23 segregated classrooms. Other local firms sent their young workers here from the 1930s; 3000 or so students attended on day release. The building is now part of Birmingham City University.

BOURNVILLE. Portion of Playground with Girls' Baths

The Bournville Village Trust was established in 1900 to relieve Cadbury of all financial interest and, in so doing, deflect unwelcome insinuations of paternalism. The Cadburys were later responsible for, amongst other things, the infants and junior school, the School of Art and the Day Continuation School. The postcard shows the female playground; this preceded the girls' recreation grounds which opened in 1896, and the baths built in 1905. It was posted in 1906 from a somewhat indignant Maud in Putney to Alice in Felixstowe, *much surprised at her news* but, nevertheless, 'sealed' with eleven kisses.

The illustration shows one of the regular week-long Initiation Schools held three times a year. The Bournville infants' school was built in 1910; a unique feature is the 48 bell carillon on the school tower – one of the finest examples of only fourteen in the country – donated by George Cadbury. It was inspired by his visit to Bruges where he was no doubt mindful of the old Flemish saying that *'Good schools and good bells are two signs of a well-managed city'*.

First Aid instruction for the girls. The sign on the back wall in Latin translates as 'nothing without God'. As with other factories of the time male and female workers were segregated with separate entrances, working, rest and dining areas and works councils. Male technicians entering areas of the factory populated by women had to wear armbands showing that they had permission to be there.

A delightful picture underscoring the importance of culture and education at Bournville. Only single women were employed in the factory; girls had to leave on marriage – but not before they were presented with a Bible and a carnation along with a talk from one of the directors. The shortage of male workers caused by the Second World War led to the first recruitment of married women. The Edwardian girls here are reading in the gardens during their lunch break – by the 1930s the works' library stock was 15,000 books and magazines – each one borrowed on average nine times per year.

George and Richard Cadbury both taught at the Birmingham Adult Schools: their progressive thinking shone through at the Bournville Continuation Classes. The photograph shows a young class enjoying lots of toys in one of the two 'Reception' classrooms built in 1938 at Bournville Infants. Further up the school, the original roll for the schools was 270 boys and 270 girls in six classrooms of 50 pupils each and six for forty. Cookery, laundry, manual instruction and handicraft classes were in the basement; the library and laboratory were in the tower; the garden was to the rear.

Cadbury was one of the first companies in the UK to introduce half day holidays. Benefits thrived in the workplace with pioneering pension schemes, a sick club, medical services, works' outings, in-service education (Continuation Classes), staff committees (the works councils) and comparatively good wages. The photograph shows the Bournville Silver Band in action at one of the regular Thursday evening dances.

A mother and her children relaxing on the village green. The Rest House is to the left – donated in 1914 by Cadbury employees to celebrate the silver wedding of George and Elizabeth Mary Cadbury in 1913. Modelled on a mediaeval butter market it houses beautiful panels depicting the history of Bournville. The shops in the background were built around 1906 but are little changed today.

The shops were built with strict regulations relating to signage and advertising which persist today. The post office moved here from Linden Road. Richard Grant bought the tobacconists and hairdresser's from Eliza Wetton in 1925. Which helps to date the photograph,

Roy's bakers van delivering his gold medal bread, while the girl in the foreground is doing backward handstands against the wall. Residents were given a rulebook laying down instructions for keeping houses and gardens in good order; it also gave advice on abstaining from alcohol on the Sabbath, and the benefits of single beds for married couples. The area was alcohol-free until 1940 with no public houses and no alcohol sold in local shops until a licensed members' bar opened in the Rowheath Pavilion. Cadbury's own research showed that one in every 30 houses in Birmingham was engaged in the sale of alcohol and that ten per cent of the city's 6,593 alcoholics died of alcohol related diseases each year. The many gin shops and gin palaces guaranteed a ready supply of mortalities but John and Candia, his wife, successfully persisted with their Total Abstinence Plan, counting even the moderate Moderation Society amongst their conquests.

John Cadbury's temperance work was only one manifestation of his attempts at social reform: it also included campaigns for workhouse reform and against industrial pollution and child labour, particularly child chimney sweeps, and animal cruelty. He founded the Animals Friend Society which evolved into the RSPCA. The picture, originally in *60 years of Planning*, is of the popular Children's Festival which took place annually. The Maypole Dance was one of the event's highlights.

Bournville was pioneering in many ways: socially, environmentally and architecturally in particular, and it also had great influence throughout Europe in such areas as housing, urban planning, community health and local education. Visitors to the village included architects from Krupp's – then in the throes of developing Essen as a company city, Dame Henrietta Barnett who inspired the development of Hampstead Garden Suburb, William Hesketh Lever who founded Port Sunlight in 1888 and the Rowntrees who built New Earswick garden village near their factory in York. Originally published in *A Century of Progress 1831-1931*, this shows commuters are arriving at the station for another day's work. The original line through Bournville in 1879 was a single line branch of the Midland Railway with the nearest station at Granville Street, half a mile away. Soon, however, this was converted to double track and extended to the new Bournville Station, now on the main Midland line through Birmingham.

All workers were enrolled in one of three pension schemes in which the company matched the employee's contribution; there were men's, women's and widow's pension plans. At the time workers' pensions were virtually unheard of. Men retired at 60, women at 55.

Cadbury was quick to recognise the value of good public relations. They set up a Visitors' Department as early as 1902 and were welcoming 150,000 people a day up to 1939 – many on organised bus or rail excursions. A two mile tour of the factory and Bournville awaited them with refreshments and a film. Only Hitler and Health & Safety stopped the flow when in 1970 regulations demanded that visitors comply to the same rigorous hygiene procedures as production line workers. But, like Hitler, Health & Safety would not get away with it. Popular demand led to the establishment of the £6 million *Cadbury World* in 1990 with 420,000 visitors going through the doors soon after opening. Research has shown that visitors were more likely to buy Cadbury confectionery products than any other up to 20 years following their visit. The picture shows the arrival of the first ever trainload of visitors.

King George VI and Queen Elizabeth visited Bournville during their visit to Birmingham on March 1st 1939. Previous royal visits took place in 1919 by George V and Queen Mary and by George VI as Duke of York in 1929. The photograph shows the Royal Procession crossing the Men's Recreation Ground – 5,000 workers enthusiastically greeted the royal party.

A high point of the day was the presentation of special caskets and Easter eggs. The King received a gold lame casket lined with white satin; the Queen's was made of gold and ivory brocade. Both contained three trays of top quality chocolates. The eggs for Margaret and Elizabeth were contained in hand-painted beige moiré silk caskets and were filled with over 70 chocolates specially decorated with either an 'M' or an 'E'. Later that afternoon the King and Queen attended a Pageant of Fitness in Birmingham Town Hall; the photograph shows the Bournville Girls' Athletic Club performing a Breton dance in traditional costume, part of a programme of national dances.

By the turn of the century sidings linked the factory with the national railway network using Cadbury rolling stock. Horse-drawn vans were the earliest mode of road transport.

Until the 1960s all the affiliated crafts and trades required to run a major chocolate manufacturing plant were carried out on site – these included the manufacture of boxes, cartons and tin cans, machine making, sheet metal production, printing, joinery, advertising and marketing. The picture shows the card box and printing department (Q Block which measured 180 x 60 metres) in full swing; the other shows 'boxing the chocolates' – in the 1950s when over 900 million chocolates were packed into boxes; 450 girls made the boxes which were transported to the packing department by electric train.

The strange construction bottom right is the Churn Tower built in 1911 at Knighton, connected to Bournville by canal. Cadbury's Dairy Milk had become the best selling chocolate brand in the UK by 1926. Cadbury's CDM website gives us some fascinating facts: *'Today, CDM remains the UK's number one chocolate brand and is worth more than £360 million. More than 65% of the British population will buy CDM at least once a year. It is also ... enjoyed by millions of people across 30 countries...Target audience: 21-29 year old females, but a great deal of interest comes from the 45 years+ consumer as well...500 million bars are made each year, in the UK. Enough of Cadbury Dairy Milk is sold every year to cover every Premiership and Nationwide league pitch – five times over. The amount of milk used in a year's production of CDM chocolate would fill 14.4 Olympic-size swimming pools'.* One pound of Cadbury milk chocolate comprises $^3/_4$ lb of chocolate and two pounds of liquid milk or, a glass and a half of full cream milk.

One of the tins, with the lower layer of chocolate intact each bar bearing the Cadbury name.

During the Boer War, Queen Victoria instructed George Cadbury to send 120,000 tins of chocolate out to the troops. At first he refused on account of his Quakerly pacifist leanings; Victoria responded tartly, pointing out that this was not a request but a royal command. The issue was resolved by splitting the order with fellow Quakers Fry and Rowntree. The tins, like the one above, were duly despatched, unbranded to obscure their origin: each tin contained 12 blocks of vanilla chocolate. George Cadbury eased his conscience by producing and sending out over one million anti-war pamphlets. The importance of chocolate in military circles was highlighted by the 1905 issue of *War Office Times & Naval Review*: '*Now chocolate is...the sweetmeat of the Services: on the march, at manoeuvres, or on any special occasion where staying power is needed.*' Fourteen years after the Boer War confectionery tins were sent to the troops in the trenches; they contained sweets, chocolates and, in a compartment at the base of Rowntrees', a set of postcards. Initially at least the fall off in demand caused by the privations of the First World War had surprisingly little impact on sales and profits – it was amply compensated for by these government orders. Nevertheless tariffs on cocoa and sugar increased and postal charges and general taxation had risen. Sugar shortages in World War One caused many brands to be shelved for the duration while others were forced into adapted recipes. Cadbury's also provided books and clothing for the troops.

Manpower shortages became critical as men joined up: at Cadbury alone 1700 out of 3000 men enlisted in the army and navy (218 did not return) with another 700 seconded to munitions work. German submarines blockaded the British Isles, forcing the government to ensure essential foods such as milk and cocoa were in good supply; this helped the chocolate companies.

Horse-drawn wagons and motor vans preparing for deliveries after 1923.

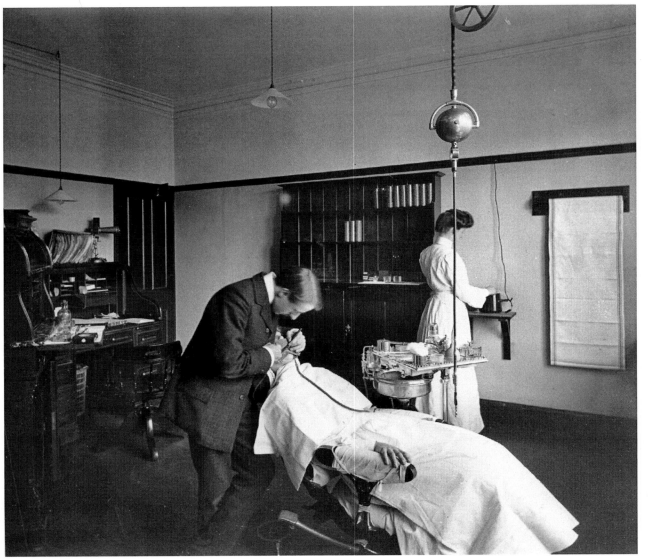

Facing page: Nurse Williams, along with two colleagues, looked after all staff (who all take a medical on joining); there are three dental surgeries with free treatment for under-18s and free tooth powder and brushes for the under-16s.

"THE DOCTOR WILL SEE YOU NOW" says NURSE WILLIAMS

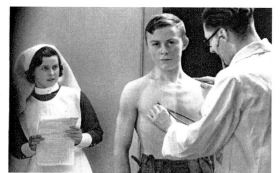

Nurse Williams and two other nurses work in Bournville's modern surgery. They can produce the health record of anyone in the factory. All new employees see the doctor before they start.

"Turn please", says Nurse Williams, and the sun-ray class moves round. Last year hundreds of regular cold-getters escaped without a sneeze. Free sun-ray is only one of four cold-prevention schemes for employees.

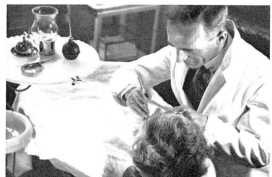

"Can I see the Dentist, please Nurse"? Which one? There are three dental surgeries on the factory. If you're under 18, treatment is free—and tooth-powder and brushes cost nothing if you're under 16.

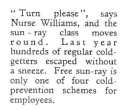

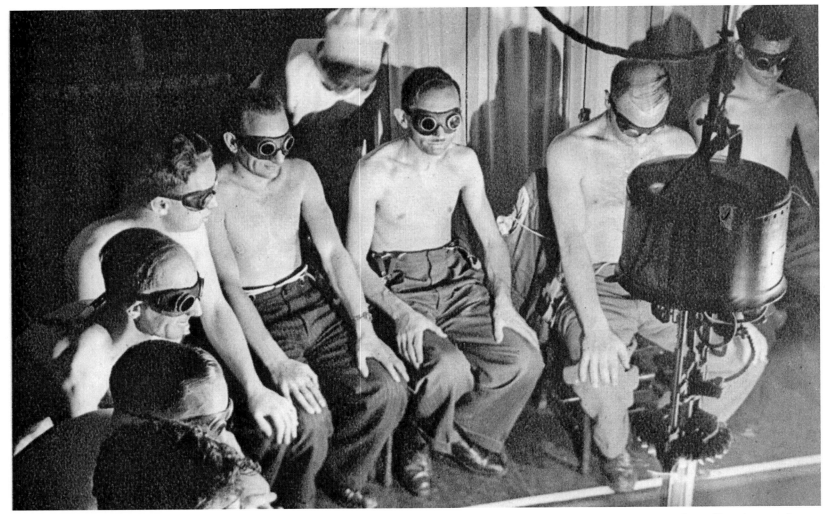

The photograph shows a free sun ray treatment session; the Bournville doctors always followed a progressive preventative policy of keeping employees healthy rather than just treating them when they were unwell. The sun-ray sessions were an example of this and one of four cold prevention schemes in the factory. *Health Hints* were circulated to all departments.

Workers making crèmes which have come direct from the melting kettles. The crèmes are made from real fruit and are made into numerous shapes using flour moulds. The all-important chocolate is then added to the centres.

The redoubtable Mrs Dee, 'dirt's worst enemy' who boasts that 'you could make chocolates in the corridor when I've finished work...men's worse than children for being untidy'.

"CALL ME FUSSY IF YER LIKE,"

says Mrs. DEE

Mrs. Dee is dirt's worst enemy. She's one of over two hundred people whose job is to keep the factory spotless. "And you could make chocolates in the *passages*" she boasts, "when I've finished work."

Fixing up the vacuum cleaner.

Vacuum or scrubbing brush, she's a demon for "thoroughness." "Men's worse than children for being untidy," she says, "'ow they'd get on without women to clean up after 'em, I don't know."

A Cadbury travelling salesman taking an order in a shop in the 1950s.

42

The busy despatch department in 1902. Men's work but in the early days women were always in the majority: apart from in 1893 numbers grew year on year and they were not outnumbered by men until 1919. Every year up to 700 women were hired although these were offset by 100 or so girls leaving to marry – the only married women employed were part-time factory cleaners. Male and female exits and entrances were so arranged that the sexes did not come into contact with each other

BOURNEVILLE - GIRLS IN DINING ROOM.

The eleven dining rooms cater for 5,000 diners every day; the dining room block built between 1918 and 1927 also houses youth club rooms and the Concert Hall seating 1,050 and, in the basement, dressing rooms for 5,000 girls. The library and doctor's and dentist's are in there too. The many clubs meet here, for example camera, chess, ambulance corps, folk dancing and 'fur and feather' – all in all 70% of employees are in one club or another.

A veritable mountain of beans. On arrival from the Gold Coast the cocoa beans are then cleaned by blasts of air and roasted for an hour in cylindrical, revolving ovens by gas jets; each oven holds 1,000 lbs of beans. The roasting releases the familiar aroma – and the husks – and become coca nibs which are then ground down. This in turn releases the cocoa butter (fifty per cent of every bean) to produce chocolate coloured, thick creamy 'mass'. 6,000 lbs of hydraulic pressure crushes the mass to extract the cocoa butter – clear and golden and used later to make solid chocolate.

Bournville's 'home guard' during the Second World War. Clearly visible here is some of the acres of camouflage made from dyed hessian which covered the factory buildings to conceal them from German aerial intelligence. The only significant damage wreaked on Bournville was on December 3rd 1940 when a bomb hit and breached the aqueduct carrying the canal over Bournville Lane causing flooding to parts of the factory and some streets. Chocolate was rationed from 1942, with three ounces allowed per person per week – half the average pre-war consumption – and supply shared between no fewer than 181 firms. Chocolate companies, or parts of them, were either transformed completely to help the war effort or else hosted other war manufacturers. In the Second World War imports of raw materials were seriously compromised; the shortages which developed as a result, and the diversion of the domestic supply of milk, affected the quality of major brands. Dairy Milk disappeared from the shops when milk was reserved for priority manufacturing use in 1941; Ration Chocolate replaced it, made from skimmed milk powder.

In 1940 Bournville Utilities Ltd was set up and 2000 employees were transferred to the new company to help the war effort: the Moulding Department produced gun doors for Spitfires, air-intake and super-charger controls for Stirlings and flare cases for other aeroplanes; Packing made the gas masks while Metals turned out pilots' seats for Defiants, junction boxes for Wellingtons and upper-mid gun turrets for Stirlings. Other departments churned out jerry cans (pictured here), fuel tanks for Spitfires, Beaufighters and Lancasters, and for Vosper motor torpedo boats.

Parts of the Bournville factory were also let to Austin for the production of aircraft gun magazines and helmets, and to Lucas to make rotating gun turrets and Sten gun magazines. Cadbury filled anti-aircraft rockets with explosives, pictured here. Of the 600 gas mask and cylinder workers a mere fifteen were men: the work required the 'nimble fingers' of women. The opening order for 5,117,039 Service Respirators and 6,335,454 canisters was completed but never used as gas warfare thankfully did not materialise. Sheep grazed on the green, 'mercy vans' with hot cocoa were sent into the Birmingham city centre during raids, the recreation fields were Dug for Victory and the Cadbury Home Guard was formed along with fire watchers, Fire and Ambulance Services and the ARP.